Dawson's Creek™

Shifting into Overdrive

by C. J. Anders

Based on the television series "Dawson's Creek™"
created by Kevin Williamson

This specially retold version by F. H. Cornish

MACMILLAN

Founding Editor: John Milne

The Macmillan Readers provide a choice of enjoyable reading materials for learners of English. The series is published at six levels – Starter, Beginner, Elementary, Pre-intermediate, Intermediate and Upper.

Level control

Information, structure and vocabulary are controlled to suit the students' ability at each level.

The number of words at each level:

Starter	about 300 basic words
Beginner	about 600 basic words
Elementary	about 1100 basic words
Pre-intermediate	about 1400 basic words
Intermediate	about 1600 basic words
Upper	about 2200 basic words

Vocabulary

Some difficult words and phrases in this book are important for understanding the story. Some of these words are explained in the story and some are shown in the pictures. From Pre-intermediate level upwards, words are marked with a number like this: ...[3]. These words are explained in the Glossary at the end of the book.

Contents

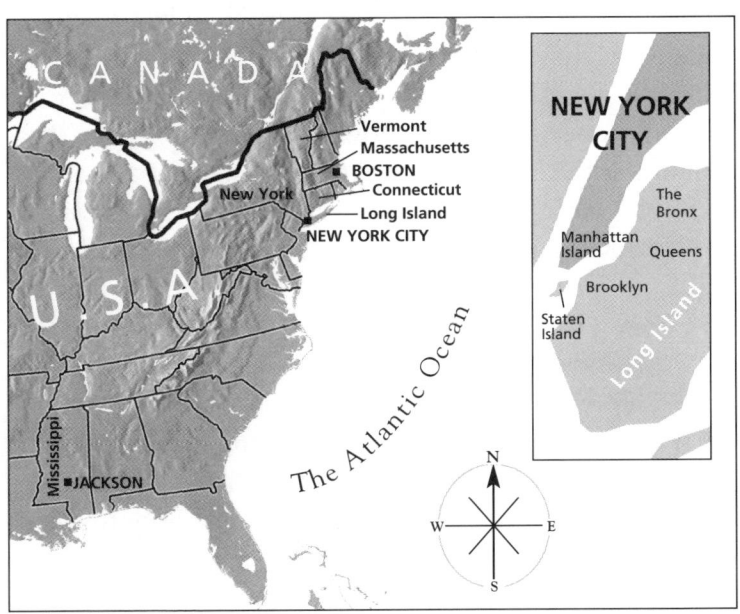

A Note About This Story

Kevin Williamson is a screenplay writer and a producer and director of movies. He was born on March 14th, 1965 and grew up in New Bern, a small town in the state of North Carolina, in the east of the U.S.A.

Kevin loved movies and his favorite director was Steven Speilberg. Kevin studied theater and film at East Carolina University. In 1987, he left New Bern and went to New York. He wanted to become an actor. When he went to Los Angeles a few years later, he worked as an assistant to a director of music videos. Kevin studied script writing and wrote screenplays for movies. The first successful movie that he wrote was *Scream* (1996). Paul Stupin worked for Columbia TriStar Television. He read the screenplay for *Scream* and he liked it. He asked Kevin to write a TV show. Kevin thought about his life in his small home town and he wrote the story for "Dawson's Creek™". The first episode of the show was made in 1997. Paul Stupin was the Executive Producer of "Dawson's Creek™".

Kevin wrote the screenplays for the movies *Scream 2* (1997), *I Know What You Did Last Summer* (1997) and *The Faculty* (1998). He wrote and directed the movie, *Teaching Mrs Tingle* (1999) and he produced the movie *Scream 3* in 2000.

The story of **"Dawson's Creek™"** takes place in a small town in the state of Massachusetts, in the northeast of the United States. The small towns and villages on the east coast have many visitors during the summer months. The tourists go fishing and they visit the restaurants. They play water sports on the sea and on the small rivers—the creeks—in the area. "Dawson's Creek™" is based on Kevin Williamson's own life when he was a teenager. He called the town in his story Capeside. The characters of Dawson and Joey are based on Kevin himself and his best friend, Fanny Norwood.

C.J. Anders is the name used by a husband and wife who are authors of fiction for young adults.

———

script the words of a movie that actors have to speak.

screenplay the script of a movie that includes all the important information for everyone who is making the movie. For example, there are instructions for the actors, cameramen and film technicians. There are descriptions of where the scenes take place.

director the person who gives instructions to everyone as a scene is filmed. The director also decides how the movie is edited before it is shown to audiences.

producer the person who is responsible for getting the money to make a movie.

The People in This Story

Dawson Leery
Age: 15
Hair: blond
Eyes: light brown
A student at Capeside High School

Family
Father: Mr Mitch (Mitchell) Leery—an architect
Mother: Mrs Gale Leery—a news presenter at a TV station

Joey (Josephine) Potter
Age: 15
Hair: long, dark brown
Eyes: brown
A student at Capeside High School

Family
Father: Mr Mike Potter—in jail
Mother: Mrs Lily Potter—dead
Sister: Bessie. Bessie and her boyfriend, Bodie, work in "The Ice House" café.
Nephew: Alexander—Bessie and Bodie's son

Pacey Witter
Age: 16
Hair: dark brown
Eyes: brown
A student at Capeside High School

Family
Father: Mr John Witter—Capeside's Chief Police Officer
Mother: Mrs Mary Witter

Brother: Doug Witter—Capeside's Deputy Police Officer
Sisters: 3

Jen (Jennifer) Lindley
Age: 15
Hair: blond
Eyes: blue
A student at Capeside High School

Family
Father: Mr Theodore Lindley—lives in New York
Mother: Mrs Helen Lindley—lives in New York
Grandmother: "Grams" (Mrs Evelyn Ryan)
Grandfather: "Gramps" (Mr Joseph Ryan)—dead

Courtney Guiliani
Age: 16
Hair: long, blond
Eyes: blue
Lives in Manhattan, New York. She is Jen's cousin.
Family
Father: William Guiliani
Mother: Grace Guiliani

Danny
Age: 18
Hair: black
Eyes: blue
Lives in New York. He meets Joey at The Cellar Café.

Abby Morgan
Age: 15
Hair: brown
Eyes: brown
A student at Capeside High School

Billy
Age: 18
Hair: dark brown
Eyes: dark brown
Lives in New York. He had been Jen's boyfriend.

Dixie
Age: 17
Hair: long, blond
Lives in Jackson, Mississippi.
She has a nephew named
Tommy. She is a ballet dancer.

**Amy, Tucker, and
Miranda**
Friends of Courtney
and Jen.
They live in New York.

Mrs Phyllis Hanover
An elderly woman who the
friends meet on the highway.

A Picture Dictionary

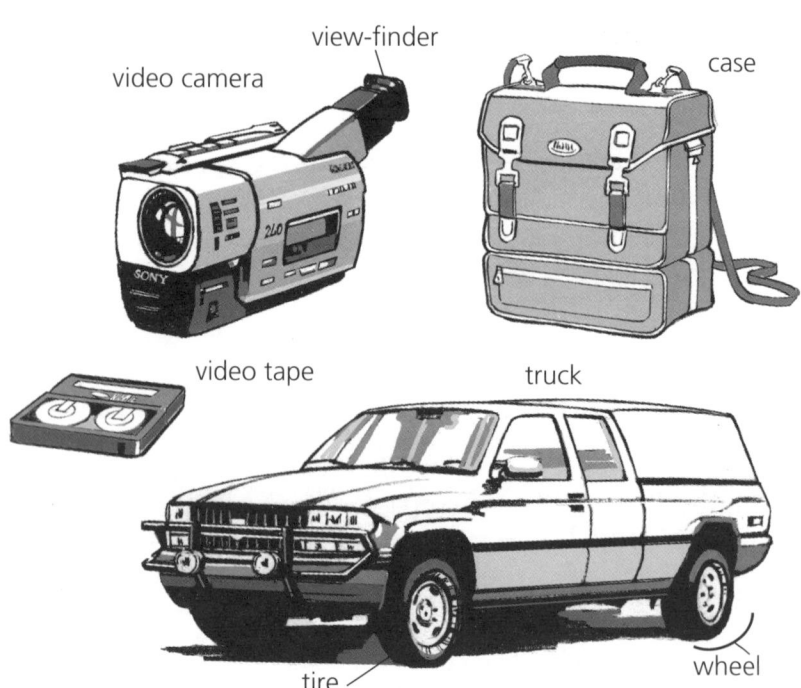

view-finder

video camera

case

video tape

truck

tire

wheel

formal dress

tuxedo

elevator

long dress

apartment building

limousine

horse and carriage

1

Life and the Movies

Joey Potter looked at her friend Dawson Leery and she smiled sadly.

"Life isn't like a movie, Dawson," she said. "We can't write happy endings to all our relationships."

Joey was a pretty girl with long brown hair. Both Joey and Dawson were nearly sixteen years old. The two teenagers had problems. All teenagers had the same problems—life, love, school work, and parents. It isn't easy to become an adult.

Dawson loved movies. He had always loved movies. He took film classes in school. He made short movies himself. Dawson wanted to be a film director. His favorite director was Steven Spielberg. Dawson spent a lot of his free time filming with his video camera. He loved watching videos of great movies from the past. Most evenings, he watched movies with Joey. And until recently, that had been fine.

But now their friendship had become difficult.

"These days, Dawson always wants us to behave like people in movies," Joey thought. And life in the little seaside town of Capeside *wasn't* like the movies.

Joey looked at the handsome, blond boy who was sitting next to her. She thought about the years of their long friendship. They had known each other all their lives. They were best friends.

Joey had always loved Dawson as a friend. But during the summer, Joey's feelings had changed. Suddenly, she'd wanted a serious relationship with Dawson. She'd wanted him to love her as a woman, not as a sister. Dawson hadn't

"Life isn't like a movie, Dawson," she said. "We can't write happy endings to all our relationships."

wanted that. He hadn't wanted to be her boyfriend. He'd wanted them to go on being best friends in the old way. Dawson hadn't wanted a serious relationship with Joey. And Joey had become very unhappy.

Then a new girl had arrived in the little town. Her name was Jen Lindley. She was a beautiful blond from New York City. She had come to live with her grandparents in Capeside. And Dawson Leery had fallen in love with her.

For a few weeks, Jen had been Dawson's girlfriend. Then she had ended that relationship. She had not wanted a serious boyfriend. Now, Dawson and Jen tried to be friends. But it was a difficult time for both of them.

Soon after Dawson's relationship with Jen ended, his feelings about Joey had changed. At last, he had fallen in love with her. And for a time, she had been his girlfriend. She had gotten what she had wanted for so long. But when she had Dawson's love, she no longer wanted it. Dawson was the only boy who she had ever known well. And now she wanted to meet new people. She no longer wanted to be close to only one person. But now Dawson was in love with her, and he didn't want her to know other boys.

Dawson and his friend Pacey Witter were still Joey's best friends. And she had started to like Jen too. The four teenagers spent a lot of time together. But life wasn't easy for any of them.

That evening, Joey had spent two hours with Dawson. Dawson had asked her to be his girlfriend again. He asked her this almost every day. They had quarrelled about it. Then they had watched a movie together. Now it was time for Joey to go home.

"Dawson, please try to leave me in peace," Joey said as she walked to the door. "I want us to be friends. But I don't want to be your girlfriend. I want to meet other guys. Maybe one of them will be my boyfriend. You have to understand that. This is my exit from the scene. Goodnight."

When she had gone, Dawson thought about Jen and Joey. He had loved both of them. But both girls had ended their relationships with him. What was wrong with him? *Why* couldn't life be like the movies?

———

The next day was Monday. In the evening, Dawson, Joey, Jen, and Pacey met in The Ice House café.

The Potter family owned the café. Joey's older sister, Bessie, and Bessie's boyfriend, Bodie, worked there too. Joey worked at the café in the evenings, after school, and on weekends.

This evening, Joey brought coffee for her three friends and she sat down with them for a few minutes.

Jen showed her friends a card with beautiful silver writing on it. It was an invitation to a party.

"The party is for my cousin Courtney's sixteenth birthday," Jen said. "It's Courtney Guiliani's sweet sixteen party. Everyone has to wear formal clothes—evening suits and long dresses. No casual clothes are allowed. I'd like to go to this party. It's going to take place in New York City, at the Plaza Hotel, on Saturday."

"Do you like your cousin?" Joey asked her. "I've never heard you talk about her."

"No, I don't like her," Jen said. "I dislike her mother too. Courtney is so *good*. She never does anything wrong. She behaves perfectly. I call her Courtney-the-Perfect. Everyone wants me to be as good as she is. Her mother, my Aunt Grace, always tells me how terrible I am. She says,

'Jennifer, you're rude and you're wild. Why can't you behave like my Courtney?' It makes me so angry."

"Then why do you want to go to Courtney's party?" Dawson asked.

"Well, it might be fun," Jen replied. "Strange things happen at parties! And I'd like to be in New York again. I miss the city! Capeside is a fine place, but it's so *quiet*. I miss New York. I miss the busy streets and the big stores. I'll phone my parents tonight. They'll know about the party. I'll say, 'I'm coming home for the weekend.' It will be great!"

———

Jen and Joey were in several classes together at school. The next day, Jen talked to Joey after a gym class.

"I talked to my parents," she told Joey. "They're going to be away from home this weekend. They're going on a business trip. But my dad said, 'You should go to your cousin's party, Jen. You could bring one of your friends from Capeside. She could stay in the apartment with you for the week-end. Then you wouldn't be lonely.' Will *you* come with me, Joey?"

At first, Joey didn't know what to say. She had never been to New York City. She wanted to see it. But Joey was very poor. Her mother was dead and her father was in jail. She and Bessie worked very hard at The Ice House. But they didn't have much money. Jen didn't understand about this problem. Her parents were very rich. She never had to worry about money.

Joey thought about all this.

"Jen, I can't come with you," she said at last. "Thank you for asking me. You're very kind. But I don't have any money and I don't have any party clothes."

"Don't worry about those things," Jen said. "I'll loan you some clothes. I have too many! And I'll pay for our train tickets to New York. I'll be happy to do that. I don't want to be alone in the apartment. We'll have fun in New York. Capeside is like a very slow car. We need to go faster, Joey. We need to have fun and excitement. We need to move up through the gears. We need to shift into overdrive!" She stopped for a moment. "Well, we certainly both need to get away from Capeside for a few days," she said.

She didn't say anything more, but she didn't *have* to say anything more.

"Yes. We both need to get away from Dawson for a few days," Joey replied. "Things aren't easy between you and him—I know that, Jen. And *I* want to be friends with Dawson again. But he won't let me be just his friend. I have to be his girlfriend or not his friend at all."

"You can never be just friends again, once you've been someone's girlfriend," Jen said. "You can't do it in real life. It isn't possible. Life isn't like the movies."

Joey laughed.

"OK, I'll come to New York with you, if Bessie will let me," she said. "Thank you, Jen."

2

The Video Store

After school, Dawson and Pacey had jobs at Screenplay Video, a video rental store. On Wednesday evening, they were both working there, putting video tapes on shelves. Dawson loved to work in the store, among all the movies. And every evening he could borrow videos from the store to play at home.

It was five o'clock and there were no customers in the store. As they worked, the two friends were talking about their unhappy lives.

Pacey's problem was his family. They didn't understand him. Pacey's father was the Chief of Police in Capeside. Pacey's older brother, Doug, was a police officer too. They were tough and difficult people. They didn't like Pacey. They didn't understand him!

Pacey didn't work hard at school. He only worked hard at things that interested him. Nothing at school interested him. His father always told him, "You're a failure, Pacey. You don't work hard. You always *say* the wrong things and you always *do* the wrong things. You're a lazy fool. I don't understand you. You're not a good son to me."

Pacey wanted to leave school and get a good job. He wanted to leave his family and live on his own.

Dawson's problem was Joey.

"Pacey, I don't want to lose her," he told his friend.

"She loves me—I'm sure of that. She isn't honest with herself. She says, 'I want to meet other boys. How will I know if you're the right boy for me if I don't meet other boys?' Pacey, I'm worried about this party that she and Jen are going to in New York. Maybe she'll meet someone there. Maybe she'll meet a tall, rich, handsome boy. Maybe she'll fall in love with him. I feel sick if I think about that, Pacey. I don't know what to do."

At that moment, someone came into the store. It was a girl from Capeside High School. Pacey and Dawson knew the teenager. They both disliked her, and she disliked them. She was always rude to them. Her name was Abby Morgan.

"I've come to return this video," Abby said. "If you guys have time to think about work, you can help me. But maybe you're too busy talking."

Abby gave the video to Pacey, then she went to look for another movie to rent. She disappeared behind some tall shelves, and Pacey and Dawson soon forgot about her.

"We both need to get away from this town for a few days," Pacey said. "Maybe *we* could go to New York for the weekend too. Then we could meet Joey and Jen. We could visit famous places with them. And they'd have to invite us to Courtney's party. You could dance with Joey. Then she wouldn't meet any tall, rich, handsome men."

"I can't follow Joey to New York," Dawson said. "She'd be so angry with me. She wants me to leave her in peace." Then he thought for a moment. "How would we get there, Pacey?" he asked. "We don't have enough money."

"Well, I've been thinking about that," Pacey replied. "My brother and my dad will be away from home this weekend. They're going to Hartford, Connecticut. They're going to a police convention—a kind of meeting for police officers. The convention is about teenage crime. I could use my dad's truck for the weekend. We could drive to New York on Friday evening and come back on Sunday."

Pacey was a little older than Dawson. He was sixteen. He had a driver's license. He was allowed to drive a car now.

"Will your dad let you borrow the truck?" Dawson asked. He was surprised.

"I won't ask him," Pacey said. "If I get back home before him on Sunday, he won't know about it."

"Is this really a good idea, Pacey?" Dawson said. He was worried.

"It's a *great* idea!" Pacey answered.

The boys had forgotten about Abby Morgan. She was still standing behind the tall shelves. She was listening to them carefully. She heard every word of their plan. And she was smiling when she quietly left the store.

3

New York

Joey and Jen arrived at the Lindleys' New York apartment on Friday evening.

The apartment was very large and very beautiful. It was at the top of a very high building, in the center of Manhattan. From the windows, there was a wonderful view of the city.

Jen picked up the phone and called a Chinese restaurant. She ordered some food.

"The restaurant will deliver the meal here," she told Joey. "We'll go out to a club after we've eaten. It will be fun."

"That will be wonderful!" Joey said. She was happy and excited. She wanted to know about life in this great city. Tonight, she was going to start learning about it.

After fifteen minutes, a delivery person brought the Chinese meal to the apartment. It was the best food that Joey had ever tasted.

Then the two girls went into Jen's bedroom and looked at her clothes. The closet where Jen kept her clothes was huge. It was bigger than Joey's bedroom in her home!

The girls quickly found some clothes which they liked. Joey put on a red dress. She also put on some of Jen's makeup. Joey didn't use makeup in Capeside, but Jen told her to wear some for the evening.

"You look wonderful!" Jen said, when she saw her friend's face.

Jen put on a short black dress and some long boots. Then she led Joey to a big mirror.

"Don't we look good?" Jen asked. "Now we'll go to a club that I know. It's called The Cellar. All my friends go there."

Jen phoned for a taxi. Joey put on a black leather jacket. Then the two girls walked to one of the elevators and went down to the street.

"Oh, Billy will be at the club," Jen told Joey, as the girls left the apartment. "You must remember Billy!" She tried to laugh. She didn't want her words to sound important.

Joey did remember Billy. He was a handsome boy. He had been Jen's boyfriend when she lived in New York. He had come to Capeside once. He'd wanted to take Jen back to the city. But at that time, Jen was in love with Dawson. She didn't want to go to New York with Billy. Billy had been angry, but he'd quickly gone away.

That had been a very sad time for Joey. Every day, she'd seen Dawson and Jen having fun together. Joey had loved Dawson herself then. She'd hated seeing him with another girl. That had hurt her very much. She remembered all this now.

"Do you *want* to see Billy?" Joey asked her friend. She was surprised.

"I want to see him, but I'm nervous about him too," Jen said. "I don't want to be his girlfriend again. But when I see him, I always have a problem. My brain tells me one thing, but my body tells me something different."

———

Half an hour later, the two girls were in The Cellar. The club was a large, rather dark room. At one end of the room, a pretty girl was standing on a brightly lit stage. She was singing. Behind her, a band was playing. People were dancing. Everyone was drinking coffee or fruit juice. The club did not sell alcohol.

Jen introduced Joey to some of her friends. One of them was a girl named Amy. And there was a boy named Tucker. Then the girls saw Billy, who was sitting in a corner. Tucker talked to Joey while Jen went over to Billy. Tucker was a friendly boy, and Joey enjoyed talking to him. The next time that she looked at Jen and Billy, they were kissing each other.

Joey was happy when she saw Jen and Billy kissing.

"Well, maybe Jen really *doesn't* want Dawson any longer," she told herself. And that made her happy. Joey didn't want Dawson to be her own boyfriend again. But she didn't want him to be *Jen's* boyfriend. When she thought about this, she was angry with herself.

"What's wrong with me?" she thought. "Dawson is my best friend. But I don't want him to be happy with me. And I don't want him to be happy with anybody else. *Why* don't I want him to be happy?"

Then something happened to Joey. She looked around her, and suddenly she saw the most handsome boy in the world. He was tall and he had black hair. He was on the other side of the room. And he was looking at her!

A few minutes later, she was dancing with him.

"My name is Danny," the boy told her. He held her very close to him as they danced. And for Joey, the world was suddenly a different place.

"This is why I need to be away from Dawson," she told herself. "I need to meet people like Danny. He's wonderful."

She smiled at the handsome young man. "My name is Joey," she said.

"Joey? But what's your real name?" he asked her softly.

And suddenly, Joey didn't want to be Josephine Potter, the poor girl from Capeside. She told some lies.

"My real name is Joelle," she said. "It's a French name. My mother is French."

"Joelle. That's a beautiful name," Danny said. "Your clothes are expensive. Your family must be very rich."

Joey didn't answer him.

"My family is very rich too," Danny said.

"Oh, Joelle!" he went on. "I want to tell you something.

22

When you came into the club with Jen, I thought, 'That girl is so lovely. She's the most beautiful girl that I've ever seen!' I *had* to talk to you. I *had* to dance with you. Do you understand?"

At that moment, a girl came into the club holding a huge basket of beautiful roses. The girl was selling the flowers for two dollars each. Danny bought all the roses and gave them to Joey.

"These are beautiful flowers for a beautiful young lady," he said. Soon he was kissing her. He kissed her again and again.

———

An hour later, Joey and Jen met in the ladies' room.

"Well, you met Danny," Jen said. "Please be careful, Joey."

"What do you mean?" Joey asked. "I don't understand."

"Well, Danny has a bad reputation—people say bad things about him," Jen replied. "He isn't a very nice guy."

"Oh, Jen, you're wrong," Joey said. "He's a wonderful guy! I've invited him back to your apartment this evening. He's talked to Billy. Billy will come with us too. Danny is ordering a big limousine to take us to the apartment. He said, 'My father will pay for it. He always pays for a limo for me.' The car will be here soon. Are you ready to leave?"

"No! Joey, don't be a fool," Jen said. "Danny will think, 'Joey wants to have sex with me.' He *always* thinks that! And Billy will think, 'Jen's going to have sex with me.' I know these people, Joey!"

"Well, maybe they *think* this," Joey said. "But it doesn't have to happen. Let's take the guys to the apartment. It will be fun!"

But Jen was right. Joey knew that as she spoke.

"No, Joey!" Jen was almost angry now. "*Listen* to me," she said. "Danny keeps a list of names. It's a list of all the girls who have had sex with him. It's a very long list. He wants to add your name to it."

Joey was shocked and unhappy.

"Find Danny quickly," Jen told her. "Tell him, 'I'm sorry. I made a mistake. We can't go back to Jen's apartment.' Then we must both get away from here."

Joey went back into the club and she found Danny. She spoke to him. At first he was angry, and so was Billy.

"I'm sorry, Danny," Joey said. "I didn't think—"

"Maybe you think too much!" Danny said.

"Well, I'm sorry," Joey said. Now she was angry too. "Maybe I thought, 'Danny's a nice boy. I'd really like to know him.' But I was wrong. I can see that now. You're not interested in people. You're only interested in sex. Please go away."

Suddenly Danny's face changed. He didn't look angry now. He looked like a little child who had done something wrong.

"Oh, Joelle, I'm sorry," he said. "Forgive me. I was wrong about you. Please, let Billy and me pick you up in the limo tomorrow evening. Billy and I are going to Courtney's party too. We'd like to take you with us."

But Joey didn't answer. At that moment, Jen joined her and the two girls left the club quickly.

"I'm sorry, Jen," Joey said. "I don't understand the big city. I didn't want to make trouble for you."

"It's OK," Jen replied. "I'll phone Billy later. I'll tell him to keep Danny away from you. I'll ask him not to pick us up from the apartment tomorrow. Please don't worry about it."

4

The Dancer
in the Parking Lot

"Oh, we *are* having fun, Pacey," Dawson said to his friend. Dawson did not mean this. He meant the opposite of what he said. He was being sarcastic.

Dawson and Pacey were sitting in the truck. They were looking at the lights in the tall buildings of Manhattan Island. They were a long way away, across a dark river. And the two friends had been traveling for many hours.

Pacey was a good driver and the journey to New York had not been difficult. But now the boys had arrived in the city, and they didn't know what to do. It was very late. They didn't know where Jen lived. They had nowhere to stay.

"It's OK," said Pacey. "Jen's parents live somewhere in Manhattan—we know that. We'll drive into Manhattan, and we'll find a parking lot. We'll sleep in the truck. Then, in the morning, we'll find Jen's apartment. We'll find her address in a Manhattan phone book."

"We'll drive into Manhattan," Pacey had said. It was easy to say it, but it wasn't easy to do it.

Neither of the boys had been to New York before. And there were so many roads. There were roads that led to bridges over the river. There were roads which led to tunnels under the river. For an hour, they were driving around in large circles.

Finally, they crossed a bridge and they were in Manhattan. But they were on a big highway. They couldn't stop anywhere on this highway, and very soon they were traveling through a tunnel. After that, they crossed another bridge. And then they were no longer in Manhattan! They didn't know *where* they were.

At last they found a parking lot. It was beside a burger restaurant. It was four o'clock in the morning and the restaurant was closed. A road sign told them where they were. They were in a place called Staten Island.

"Maybe I'll kill you," Dawson told his friend. "But I can't drive the truck home. So maybe I'll let you live till Monday! Let's try to sleep."

_____

It was six thirty when Dawson woke. The sky was beginning to get light. Dawson tried to wake Pacey.

"Go away," Pacey said. "I don't want to go to school. Let me sleep!"

Dawson got out of the truck. He was cold and hungry. His body was stiff and tired. As he looked around, he saw lights in the restaurant. Someone was switching them on, one by one. The restaurant was opening for the day.

Dawson went into the restaurant and bought some food and some coffee.

When he'd finished his breakfast, he went outside and walked back towards the truck. Many cars were coming into the parking lot now. One of them was an old blue Ford. A blond girl was driving the car. She was the most beautiful girl that Dawson had ever seen. In the car with her was a little boy with red hair.

The girl and the little boy got out of the old Ford. The boy jumped in the air.

"I want a milk shake! I want a *big* milk shake," he shouted. "I want a milk shake, then I want some ice cream."

"Please, stop shouting," the girl said. Dawson listened to her voice. Her accent was very different from the accent of this northeast part of the U.S. This girl came from one of the southern states. Dawson had never heard such a beautiful voice.

"Your mom will be angry if you have a milk shake and ice cream for your breakfast, Tommy," the girl said.

Dawson was interested in these words. "She isn't the boy's mother," he said to himself. "Maybe she's his nanny."

Dawson had known an Australian girl who was a nanny. She had worked for a family in Capeside during the summer. She'd taken care of their new babies.

The little boy with red hair wasn't happy.

"It's my birthday," he said angrily. "I can have anything that I want today—you told me that!" Then he started shouting again.

"Milk shake! Milk shake! Milk shake!" he shouted.

"OK, Tommy, OK, OK," the beautiful blond girl said. "If you stop shouting, you can have *ten* milk shakes!"

"Great!" the boy said.

As they walked towards the restaurant, Dawson watched them. The girl moved so gently and so beautifully. He got his video camera from the truck and he started to film the two of them. The girl saw him, and she stopped. She held the little boy's hand and she led him towards Dawson. Dawson stopped filming.

"What were you doing?" the girl asked Dawson in a beautiful soft voice.

"I was filming you," Dawson said. "I saw you get out of your car. You're so beautiful, and you move so beautifully. I *had* to film you. Are you angry with me?"

The girl smiled.

"No, I'm not angry," she said. "Thank you for saying nice things about me. Do you live in New York?"

"No, I live in Capeside, Massachusetts," Dawson told her. "My friend and I drove here last night. My friend is in the truck. We're going to visit someone—someone he knows. My name is Dawson."

The girl smiled again. "My name is Dixie," she replied. She held out her hand. "I live in Jackson, Mississippi. I'm staying in New York for a few days with my sister. This is her little boy. His name is Tommy."

Dawson held Dixie's hand and shook it. Then he shook Tommy's hand.

"I'm a dancer," Dixie said. "I've been studying ballet for many years. I want to join a ballet company in this city. I danced for the director of the company yesterday. He didn't hire me. I have to try again next year. I was sad because I want to be a professional dancer. I'm a good dancer. I want to work with a famous ballet company. Do you want to see me dance?"

Before Dawson could answer, Dixie was dancing around the parking lot. She jumped into the air. She spun around and around. She *was* a very good dancer. Dawson filmed her on video tape while she danced.

"You were wonderful," he told Dixie, when she stopped moving. "You will be a very famous dancer one day."

"Well, that's what I dream about," Dixie said. "I've always dreamed about that. But sometimes I feel stupid. Maybe dreams *are* stupid."

"No!" said Dawson quickly. "Dreams *aren't* stupid. A dream is something that nobody can take away from you. All great people start with nothing but a dream!"

Dixie smiled at him. And Dawson wanted to say more. But Tommy wanted his breakfast.

"Can we go now, Dixie?" the little boy asked. "I'm so hungry."

"OK, Tommy," Dixie said. "We have to go now," she told Dawson.

"Can I see you again?" he asked her.

"I'm going back to Jackson tomorrow," she replied. "So we won't meet again. But it was good to meet you this morning. Thanks, Dawson. Thanks for what you said about dreams."

A moment later, Dixie had gone into the restaurant with the little boy.

Dawson felt sad. For a few minutes, a girl had changed his life. But he was never going to see Dixie again and that made him very sad.

At that moment, Pacey got out of the truck. He looked at his friend's face.

"What's wrong with you?" he asked.

Dawson tried to explain his feelings, but Pacey didn't understand.

"Dawson," he said. "Last week you were worried about Joey. You were worried because she might meet another guy this weekend. You didn't want to lose her. Now *you've* met another girl, and the world has changed for you. Are you worrying about losing Joey now? No! You're worried because you've lost a blond who you knew for only ten minutes. Dawson, the world is full of blonds. The world is full of girls. This is real life, not a movie, my friend!"

Pacey went into the restaurant for some breakfast. Dawson stayed in the truck.

"I don't want to see Dixie again, and then lose her again," he told himself. "The memory of her is perfect. I'll keep the memory. And I'll always have my film of her."

When Pacey came out of the restaurant, the boys drove back into Manhattan, and finally they found a parking lot there. Then they rode on the subway—the underground railway—to Grand Central Station. There, they found a Manhattan phone book. They found the phone numbers of everyone in the city named Lindley.

"But we don't know Jen's father's first name," said Dawson. "We'll never find her parents' address. This was another stupid idea, Pacey."

They called all the Lindleys whose numbers were in the phonebook. None of them knew Jen.

"What are we going to do now?" Dawson asked.

"Well, we know one thing," said Pacey. "Jen's cousin's party is going to take place at the Plaza Hotel, this evening. We'll be tourists today. We'll visit the famous buildings in the city. Then this evening, we'll go to the hotel. There'll only be one sweet sixteen party for a girl named Courtney there. We'll find Jen and Joey at the party."

"Wonderful!" said Dawson. "But I'm still going to kill you on Monday!"

5

Rumors

Jen and Joey spent most of Saturday visiting famous places in the city. Joey had never been to New York before. Jen took her to the Statue of Liberty. She took her to the top of the Empire State Building. She took her to some expensive stores. She took her to wonderful cafés, where they had coffee and lunch. Jen paid for everything. Joey was very worried about this, but Jen was happy to do it.

"Please don't worry,

Joey," she said. "It's good to spend time with you away from Capeside."

"And it's good to spend time away from Dawson Leery," Joey said. "We both need time away from Dawson."

Everything was wonderful until they met one of Jen's New York friends. Jen and Joey saw the girl on the other side of a street that they were walking down. She was coming towards them.

"That's a girl named Miranda," said Jen. "She's a horrible person. I've known her for most of my life. And I've disliked her for most of my life too! She spreads rumors about people—she tells lies about them. She always has a nasty story to tell me about someone that I know. And she always has a nasty story to tell *them* about *me*."

Miranda was a small thin girl with brown hair. Her clothes looked very expensive. She crossed the street and she stopped Jen and Joey.

"Hi, Jen," the girl said. "Billy told me about your visit to The Cellar."

"Hello, Miranda," Jen said. "This is my friend, Joey."

"Hello, Joey," Miranda said. Then she turned back to Jen. "How is your problem?" Miranda asked her. "Are you feeling better these days?"

"I don't understand you," Jen replied. "What problem?"

"Your alcohol problem, Jen," Miranda said. "Everybody knows about it. Weren't you in the hospital getting treatment? You've been away from home for a long time."

"No, I was *not* in the hospital!" said Jen angrily. "And I didn't have an alcohol problem."

"Oh, well—that's good," said Miranda. "But that was the story that *I* heard."

"The story was wrong," said Jen. "It was like most of the

stories that *you* hear, Miranda."

"Are you going to Courtney's sweet sixteen party tonight?" Miranda asked.

"Yes, we'll be there," Jen said. "Why do you ask, Miranda?"

"Well, I *did* hear another story," Miranda said. "Maybe you need to hear it before you go to the party."

"And what was *this* nasty story?" Jen asked.

"It's about Billy and Courtney," Miranda said. "They've been having sex together for months."

A few seconds later, Miranda had walked away.

Jen was angry. "It can't be true," she told Joey. "Billy hates Courtney. He's *always* hated her."

"Then you're right," Joey said. "The story can't be true. But why do you care? You don't want Billy to be your boyfriend any more. You told me that."

"I don't want him as a *boyfriend*," Jen replied. "But I do want him as a *friend*. I want to be good friends with him."

"Listen, Jen," Joey said. "Last week you were talking about me and Dawson. You said, 'You can never be just friends again once you've been someone's girlfriend.' You told me that."

"This is different," Jen said. "Dawson was your friend before he was your boyfriend. Billy was *never* an ordinary friend to me."

And when Jen thought about what she had said, it made her very sad.

—————

In Capeside that evening, Doug Witter, Pacey's brother, walked into The Ice House. He sat down at a table. Bessie came over to him and he ordered some coffee. At the next table, Doug saw a teenaged girl.

"Hi," the girl called to him. "My name is Abby Morgan. I'm in some classes with Pacey at school. Pacey is my friend. Why aren't you in Hartford this weekend at the police convention on teenage crime?"

"I had to come back early," Doug said. "Two of the officers in my group are sick. I have to do their jobs tomorrow. My dad is still at the convention. But how did you know about it?"

Abby smiled.

"Oh, Pacey told me about it," she answered. "He told me, 'My brother and father are away for the weekend. I'm going to borrow my dad's truck. I'm going to drive to New York with Dawson Leery.' That's how I knew about the convention."

Doug stood up. He put some money on his table and he left the café. He didn't finish his coffee.

A few minutes later, he talked to his father on the phone.

"Pacey has to be punished," thought Doug as he put the phone down. "He's told lies and he's taken Dad's truck without permission. He's a bad son to his father. I'm a *good* son. And I've done what a good son has to do. I've told the truth."

6

Sweet Sixteen

Jen and Joey were standing in front of the mirror in Jen's bedroom. They had spent two hours getting ready to go to Courtney's party. Joey was wearing one of Jen's formal dresses. It was a long dark blue dress. It was very beautiful and very expensive. Jen had also found a bracelet with blue jewels, and Joey was wearing this too. Her dark hair was clean and shiny.

But Jen was not wearing a long, formal dress. Her pale blue dress was very short and it was made of silk.

"Well, I already have a bad reputation in this city," she told Joey. "Everybody here thinks, 'Jen's a bad girl.' So I've decided to *look* like a bad girl!"

"You told Danny and Billy not to pick us up with a limo," Joey said to Jen. "Did they listen to you? Will they do what you asked them to do?"

"I don't know," Jen replied. "We'll soon find out about that."

The two girls put on their coats. Then they left the apartment and went down in an elevator to the street. Outside the building they had a big surprise. Danny and Billy *were* waiting for them. The boys were wearing black tuxedos—formal evening suits. But they hadn't arrived in a limo. They hadn't come in *any* kind of car. They had arrived at the apartment building in a carriage which was pulled by a horse. The carriage was gold and the horse was white. The driver wore a white suit and a gold hat.

"You girls look wonderful tonight," Danny said. "Please let us take you to the party in our carriage."

Jen and Joey talked quietly for a few moments.

"OK," Jen said at last. "We'll come with you. But we aren't going to be with you all the evening. Don't make any plans for us."

"OK," the boys said together.

They all got into the carriage.

At first, the girls were nervous. They were worried about the two boys. *Did* they have plans for the evening? But after a few minutes, they stopped worrying. The girls enjoyed the ride to the party.

"Are you having fun, Joelle?" Danny whispered to Joey.

"Yes, this is great," she answered. She couldn't be angry with him any longer. He was so handsome and so rich.

And he liked her so much—she could see that!

"Joelle, please, let's forget about last night," he whispered. "I behaved badly—I know that. But I'm so sorry about it."

"OK, Danny," she said. "Let's forget about it."

———

Joey and Jen looked around them. They were in the room where the party was taking place. They had left Billy and Danny at the entrance to the hotel, and now the girls were walking into the Rose Room.

The Rose Room at the Plaza Hotel was amazing! It was huge. In one part of the room there were large tables with white cloths on them. Ten people could sit at each table. And there were other tables with dishes of food on them. In the middle of one table were some large letters made of ice. The letters said COURTNEY'S SWEET SIXTEEN. The girls left their coats with a clerk and walked further into the room.

The room was full of people. In one corner, an orchestra was playing dance music. Many of the guests at the party were dancing to the music.

"Your aunt and uncle must have spent thousands of dollars on this party," Joey said. "They must be very rich."

"Oh yes," Jen replied in a cold hard voice. "They *are* very rich—and they like everyone to know that."

Joey looked around the room again. Near one wall there was a big white screen. Every few seconds, a color photo appeared on this screen. All the photos were of Courtney. Some photos showed her when she was a baby. Some showed her when she was a young child. Some showed her when she was a young teenager. There were photos for every year of her life.

"Look behind you, Joey," Jen said.

On the wall behind her, Joey saw a large painting. It was ten feet high.

"It looks like the *Mona Lisa*—Leonardo da Vinci's famous portrait of an Italian woman," Joey thought.

But the painting was much bigger than Leonardo's picture. And the woman in the portrait had Courtney's face! Somebody had painted the picture specially for the party.

Suddenly, a tall slim girl came towards them. She had straight blond hair and she was wearing a long dress. The dress was pink and white. It looked very expensive.

"Cousin Jen!" the girl called.

"This must be Courtney-the-Perfect," Joey told herself.

"Oh, you must be Jen's little friend from Capeside," the blond girl said to Joey. Then she turned back to Jen. The two cousins did not look happy to see each other.

"Well, you *are* brave," Courtney said to Jen. "*I* couldn't wear a dress like that tonight. But was it a good idea, Jen? My friends will think, 'Courtney was wrong. Jen's still a bad girl.' I told everyone about your new life in Massachusetts. I said, 'Jen has changed. She's a nice, sensible girl now.' Will they believe me when they see you in that dress?"

At that moment, Billy came over to them. He kissed Courtney and she smiled at him.

"Are you going to dance with me later?" she asked.

"Yes, my birthday girl," he replied. "I want that more than anything in the world. But first, I want to find some alcohol. In this room, there's only apple juice."

"Oh, my mother decided about that," Courtney said. "She's making me so angry today!"

"Well, Danny is looking for a better drink for us," Billy

told her. "I'll see you again soon."

Billy kissed Courtney again. Then she moved away from them. She was going to talk to someone else.

"Ugh!" Jen said.

"She still makes you feel bad," said Billy.

"How does she make *you* feel, Billy?" Jen replied. "That's the important question!"

"I–I don't understand you," Billy said quickly. But his face became red and he turned away from her. "I'm going to find Danny," he said.

As he walked away, a woman in a gray silk dress came towards the girls. She was a beautiful middle-aged woman. Her dress looked very expensive.

"Jennifer!" the woman called. Jen hated her full name. Everybody else called her "Jen" because that was the name that she liked.

"Hello, Aunt Grace," Jen said. "I must introduce you to Joey. This is my friend Joey Potter, from Capeside. Joey, this is my aunt—Grace Guiliani. She's Courtney's mother."

The woman held Joey's hand for a moment, then she started to talk to Jen.

"Where are your parents, Jennifer?" she asked.

"They're away from New York," Jen replied. "They had to go on a business trip."

Aunt Grace looked angry. "Was their stupid business trip more important than my daughter's party?" she asked. "Well, they never think about anybody but themselves. They've never taken care of *you*, Jen. That's the reason why you've always been so wild."

"Yes, Aunt Grace," Jen replied in a cold hard voice. "You must be right. But not everyone can have a wonderful mother like Courtney's."

Jen was angry and she was being sarcastic—she meant the opposite of what she said. But her aunt didn't understand this.

"Well, you're right about that, dear," she said happily. Then suddenly, she was angry again. "Why are you wearing that dress?" she asked. "Everyone must wear formal clothes this evening. That was written on the invitations. Are you trying to ruin my little girl's party? That's a terrible thing to do!"

"I'm wearing this dress because I like it," Jen replied coldly. "Will you take me to see my Uncle William now, please? I haven't seen him yet."

When Jen and her aunt had gone, Joey saw a young man walking towards her.

"Hello, Joey," he said. "We met at The Cellar last night. You look beautiful tonight. Will you dance with me?"

It was the young man named Tucker. Joey started to dance with him. He was a very good dancer. He wasn't handsome like Danny, but he was kind and funny. He didn't hold Joey too close to him. She enjoyed talking to him and she enjoyed dancing with him. She wanted to dance with him again later.

When the music finished, Joey and Tucker sat down. Joey saw Miranda walking towards them. She was with Jen's friend, Amy.

"Hi, Joelle," Miranda said. "Where did you get that terrible dress. It looks cheap."

"Are you trying to be rude to me, Miranda?" Joey asked her. "Was that an insult? Maybe it was. I'm not sure about it, because it wasn't really clever enough for an insult."

Miranda's face became red and Amy laughed at her.

"Are you trying to be rude to me, Miranda?"

"Tell me, Joelle," Miranda said angrily. "Is the rumor about you true? Did you have sex with Danny last night, one hour after you first met him? Is the story true? Everybody here believes it!"

7

The Wrong Clothes

Dawson and Pacey came out of a subway station and walked towards the Plaza Hotel. They were wearing casual shirts and blue jeans. Dawson was carrying his video camera. The boys' shirts were clean, but they had been wearing their jeans since Friday morning. They weren't correctly dressed for a formal party.

"I'm worried, Pacey," Dawson said to his friend. "No one invited us to this party. Maybe the people at the hotel won't let us go in. If they do let us go in, maybe the girls will be angry with us."

"Dawson, you worry too much," Pacey said. He laughed. "You wanted to be with Joey this weekend. Now I've brought you here. Are you happy? No—you're worrying about everything. Be calm, Dawson. Everything will be OK. I'm right. I'm *always* right—you know that."

"Pacey," Dawson replied. "Don't be a fool. When you have to choose what to do, you *always* do the wrong thing. Everyone knows that. You have a reputation for it. You always do and say the wrong things."

The two boys entered the hotel. Pacey walked over to the reception desk. A man was sitting behind it. He was the reception clerk—he helped guests and visitors.

"There's a sixteenth birthday party here tonight," Pacey said to the clerk. "Where can we find it?"

"Maybe you've made a mistake, young man," the reception clerk told him. "There *is* a party here tonight, in the Rose Room. But the people at *that* party are all wearing formal clothes. It can't be the party that you are looking for."

"OK," Pacey said. "I'm sorry. Maybe we *did* come to the wrong place."

He walked away from the reception desk, towards the elevators. Dawson followed him. A minute later, they were entering the Rose Room. The room was full of men wearing tuxedos and women wearing long, formal dresses. An orchestra was playing old-fashioned dance music. It was not the kind of music that most teenagers like!

A young woman with long red hair came over to the two boys. She looked at their clothes.

"Hello," she said. "Can I help you? Maybe you've come to the wrong party."

Dawson thought quickly. He held up his video camera.

"I'm the videographer," he said. "My name is Mr Leery. This is my assistant, Mr Witter. We work for a company called Screenplay Video. Courtney's parents asked Screenplay Video to make a film of the party. The company sent us here to make the film."

"Didn't the company tell you that this was a formal party?" the girl asked them.

"Well, Screenplay Video is a big company," Pacey replied. "Maybe we didn't get the complete information."

"Well, if you know about Courtney, you must be OK," the girl said. "Please start filming." And she walked away.

Dawson lifted the camera to his face and looked through the viewfinder. He shot a few seconds of film.

"Well, we got into the party. Now let's find Joey and Jen," Pacey whispered to him.

But at that moment the boys heard a voice behind them.

"Who are you boys? Why are you here?" the voice asked.

Dawson and Pacey turned around. A beautiful middle-aged woman in a gray silk dress was talking to them. And next to her was a tall man in a tuxedo. On the man's coat was a badge. The words on the badge were JOSEPH SARRAT VIDEO SERVICES—J. SARRAT, VIDEOGRAPHER.

The woman was looking angrily at Dawson and Pacey.

"This is my daughter's party," the woman said. "And this is the gentleman who I asked to make a film of the party. So what are *you* doing here? If you don't tell me, I'll send for the hotel security staff. And they'll call the police!"

———

Joey was very, very angry. For half an hour, she had been looking for Danny. She hadn't found him yet.

"When I *do* find him, I'll get the truth from him," she told herself. "Did he tell lies about me to Miranda and his other friends? Did he say, 'I had sex with Jen's friend last

45

night.' If he told them that, I'll *kill* him!"

But Joey couldn't find Danny anywhere. And she couldn't find Jen or Billy either. She was angry with Danny, but she was angry with Jen too.

"Jen is not a good friend," she thought. "She brought me here, then she left me alone. She left me with hundreds of people who I don't know. I'm going to find Danny. I'm going to get the truth from him. Then I'm going to leave this horrible place!"

A few minutes later, she saw Tucker again. She smiled at him.

"Hi," she said.

"Oh, hi," he replied sadly. "I'm looking for some friends. Maybe I'll see you later." And he walked quickly away.

"He doesn't want to talk to me," Joey thought sadly. "He believes the rumors about me and Danny."

Joey went to the clerk where she had left her coat. She didn't want to find Danny now. She didn't want to stay here any longer. She didn't have any money. But she decided to walk back to Jen's apartment. "That will be better than staying here a minute longer," she told herself. But as she put her coat on, she heard a voice behind her.

"J–Joelle, w–where are you going? I've been l–looking for you." It was Danny's voice. His voice was not clear—it was slurred. He had drunk a lot of alcohol—Joey knew that. She turned around and looked at him. She looked at him with anger and hate.

"I've been looking for you too," she said. "Did you tell lies about me to your horrible friends? There's a rumor about me here. Everyone has heard it. The rumor is, 'Jen's friend, Joey, had sex with Danny last night. She had sex with him an hour after she first met him.' So I want to know something, Danny. Did *you* start this rumor?"

"Well, yes," Danny replied. He laughed. "I've had lots of girlfriends. I can have sex with anyone I want. Everyone knows that—that's my reputation. I want everyone to believe my reputation. You don't want me to lose my reputation, Joelle." He laughed again.

"You are a horrible liar," Joey said quietly. "If you ever say my name again, to *anybody*, I will know about it. And if I know that, I will make you very, very unhappy. Now go away!"

Joey pushed Danny hard and he almost fell over. Then she turned towards the door. But as she reached the door, she heard people shouting. She heard a voice that she knew well.

"We made a mistake," the voice said nervously. "We were hired to make a film of a sweet sixteen birthday party. We came to the wrong party—that's all that happened. We're sorry. We'll leave now."

It was Dawson!

Joey closed her eyes. "Oh, no! This can't be happening to me!" she told herself.

Dawson and Pacey, dressed in jeans and casual shirts, were standing in the middle of a crowd of angry people. Joey saw Amy and Miranda in the crowd. And she saw Jen's aunt and Courtney too.

"I don't believe you. I'm going to call the police, now!" Aunt Grace shouted.

Joey looked at the two boys. "They followed us here," she told herself. "Dawson won't leave me alone. This is terrible! I'm so angry with him!"

This was true. But Joey was angry with Jen and her friends and family too. Suddenly she knew what to do.

She spoke to Jen's aunt.

"Don't call the police," she said. "This is my mistake. *I* invited them here."

"*You* invited them?" Aunt Grace shouted. "Why?"

Courtney was standing next to her mother. She looked angrily at Joey.

"It's *my* party," Courtney said. "Why did you invite people to it? I don't know you. *Nobody* here knows you!"

"Well, *Danny* knows her," Miranda said in a cold, cruel voice. "He knows her *very* well. Lots of boys know her very well. Isn't that true, Joelle?"

People in the crowd laughed.

At that moment, Jen arrived. She looked around her. Quickly she understood what was happening.

"Your horrible friend invited these terrible boys to my daughter's party," Aunt Grace said to her. "Poor people from bad families do that kind of thing. Take her away from here!"

"No, that's wrong, Aunt Grace," Jen said calmly. "Joey didn't invite them. *I* invited them."

Courtney screamed. "You did this to ruin my party!" she shouted at Jen. "I hate you!"

Suddenly Dawson spoke.

"Jen and Joey didn't know about this," he said to Jen's aunt. "They didn't invite us—that is the truth. We followed them here. We apologize Courtney—we're very sorry. We'll leave when *you've* apologized to Jen."

"You must be crazy!" Courtney shouted. "I'm not going to apologize to *her*. I hate her. I've always hated her!"

Then Joey heard another voice. It was a very slurred voice. It was Danny's voice.

"J–Joelle," Danny said. He almost fell over as he walked

up to her. "Y–you're still here. You couldn't leave without me." He laughed and he looked around at his friends. "Joelle couldn't leave without me," he told them.

"You're a liar and you're drunk," Joey said quietly. "I told you never to say my name again." Then she hit Danny very hard across the face. He fell to the floor.

"I think the movie ends here," Dawson said. "It's time for our exit from this scene." He held Joey's arm and Pacey held Jen's arm. The four friends walked out of the room.

8

Pacey Does the Right Thing

The next day, the four friends were sitting in Pacey's father's truck. They were on their way home to Capeside. They had stayed the night at Jen's apartment. But now they had to get back home.

"I have to be home before my dad and my brother get back from the police convention on teenage crime," Pacey told the girls. "They didn't know about this trip to New York. I borrowed the truck. But I didn't ask them first."

There weren't many cars on the road but the weather was terrible. Rain was falling heavily. Pacey had to drive slowly.

The four teenagers didn't say much. Each of them was thinking.

Jen was thinking about the angry phone call that she'd had from her aunt that morning.

"You ruined my daughter's party," her aunt had told her angrily. "You brought that horrible girl from Capeside. The young man that she hit spent the night in a hospital. We had to go there with him. When your horrible friend hit him, she broke his nose. And *you* are as bad as she is. I know all about you, young lady! I know—"

"Goodbye, Aunt Grace," Jen had said. And she had put the phone down in the middle of her aunt's sentence.

When Billy had phoned Jen a little later, she had done the same thing. She hadn't listened to him. She'd put the phone down while he was still speaking.

"Going back to New York was a mistake," she told herself now. "It was a *big* mistake."

Joey was thinking about Dawson. Before they went to their bedrooms the night before, she'd told him a lot of things. She was angry about what he had done. She had told him this.

"You have to leave me alone, Dawson," she had said. "You have to leave me in peace. I've told you that before. I want to meet other boys. All my life, I've only known you. Are you the right person for me? I won't know about that until I've known some other boys."

"I made a mistake this weekend—I know that," she went on. "I saw Danny at a club and suddenly my life changed. It happened in a moment. I didn't have a choice about it. I didn't choose to feel like that about him. But when I saw him, I *wanted* to spend time with him. I felt excited about him. Danny was dangerous and he made me nervous. That excited me. He wanted to be with me very much. I didn't understand what he really wanted from me."

"I don't want to hear about Danny," Dawson had said.

"You *must* hear about him," Joey had replied. "I *need* to tell you about him. I made a mistake. I chose the wrong guy. But I have to make my own mistakes, Dawson. You can't control my life. Please don't try to do that."

Then she'd looked at her best friend—the boy who she had loved since they were children. Suddenly, she'd felt very sorry for him.

"I'll always be your friend, Dawson," she'd said. "But at this time, we must only be friends and no more than that."

"I like you, Dawson," Joey had continued. "I love you, in a special way. If I lost your friendship, I'd be terribly unhappy. But I don't want to be your girlfriend. I don't want you to be angry with me all the time. I want to tell you about the other people I meet. I want to tell you about my feelings for them. I want us to be honest with each other. I want you to be my best friend again. Do you understand?"

"I understand, Joey," Dawson had replied sadly. "You want me to forget my feelings for you. You want me to be someone who you can talk to. You want to tell me about the people who are in love with you. I can't be that kind of friend for you, Joey. I'm sorry. Goodnight." And he'd turned and left the room.

Joey had been surprised. She always chose the exits from their scenes together. She always spoke the last words in their scenes. But last night, she hadn't been able to say any more.

Joey was thinking about that as Pacey drove the truck carefully back towards their little seaside town. And Dawson was thinking about it too. And he was also thinking about Dixie, the pretty girl from the parking lot in Staten Island.

"If I could see Dixie again, maybe I wouldn't think about Joey all the time," he thought.

Pacey was thinking about his father and his brother. His thoughts weren't happy either.

"Why do I worry about behaving badly?" he asked himself. "If I behaved perfectly every day for a year, Dad and Doug still wouldn't like me. They'd still say, 'Pacey, you're a fool. And you're a failure.' They don't really care what I do, because they don't really care about *me*. They enjoy making my life difficult. They enjoy punishing me."

The four friends were thinking their own thoughts as Pacey drove the truck through the rain.

Suddenly, the truck slowed down. Pacey was stopping. A car had broken down at the side of the highway. A small, elderly woman was standing next to it. She was looking very unhappy and she was getting very wet.

Pacey looked at his watch.

"We can help this lady and we can still get back to Capeside before my dad," he told the others. "We can't leave her by her broken down car."

Pacey stopped the truck and he and Dawson got out. They ran over to the elderly woman.

"Thank you for stopping," she said. "You're very kind. I forgot to bring my phone with me. I can't call a garage. Oh, my name is Phyllis Hanover."

Pacey and Dawson introduced themselves. Then they looked at the car. One of its tires was flat. There was a hole in the rubber and all the air had gone.

"Is there a spare wheel in the car?" Pacey asked the woman. "If there is, we'll change the wheel for you."

But when they got the spare wheel from the back of the woman's car, its tire was flat too.

"Oh no," the woman said. "The spare needed repairs. I forgot. I'm so stupid. What shall I do?"

The woman was getting wetter and wetter. Her coat wasn't waterproof—the rain was getting through it. Dawson saw this. He helped her remove her wet coat. Then he put his own waterproof jacket around her shoulders. While Dawson was doing this, Pacey went to talk to the girls in the truck. Soon they had made a decision. They all walked over to the lady's car.

"This is what we'll do, Mrs Hanover," Pacey told the elderly lady when he returned. "Joey and Dawson will wait here in your car. They will look after it for you. You and Jen and I will take your spare wheel and we'll go in my truck. We'll look for a garage which can repair your spare tire. Then we'll bring you back here and put the wheel on the car for you."

———

Five minutes later, Pacey and Jen were driving in the truck with Mrs Hanover. They were looking for a garage.

"The nearest garage is a long way from here," Mrs Hanover said. "This is so kind of you. Where do you come from, Pacey?"

"I live in Capeside, Massachusetts," Pacey replied. "We all live there."

"Pacey's father is the Chief of Police in Capeside," Jen told the woman. "We've spent the weekend in New York, and now we're going home."

"And I'm making you late," Mrs Hanover said. "I'm sorry. You're all very kind."

———

Joey and Dawson were sitting in Mrs Hanover's car. They were trying to keep warm. They were both unhappy. They didn't want to talk about themselves, so they talked about Pacey.

"I was surprised when Pacey stopped to help that woman," Joey said. "He has to get home before his father arrives. If we're late, he'll be in terrible trouble. Pacey knows that. But he stopped to help someone."

"Yes, I was surprised too," Dawson replied. "He had to choose what to do. And for the first time in his life, Pacey did the right thing!"

Joey looked at him.

"Well, maybe it will be *your* turn soon, Dawson," she said. "Maybe *you'll* do the right thing too. Maybe *you'll* make the right choice." And she smiled at him.

9

Home Again

Dawson opened the door of his house, took off his wet coat, and went into the living room. His parents were waiting for him there. They were watching TV, but his father switched it off when Dawson entered.

"Well, Dawson, did you have a good weekend at *Pacey's* house?" Mr Leery asked.

Dawson sat down. He was in trouble—he knew that. Pacey's father must have phoned his parents already.

"Dad, Mom, I'm sorry," the boy said. "I told you a lie. We weren't at Pacey's house. We went to New York City. Joey and Jen went there for a party. We wanted to be with them."

"You wanted to *follow* them," Dawson's father said. "So you and Pacey stole Mr Witter's truck and you went to New York. Are you crazy?"

"Maybe I *am* crazy," Dawson replied sadly. "I don't know. But I was wrong to do what I did. I know that now. I'm very sorry."

"Dawson, we have to punish you," Mr Leery said. "We're going to do the only thing that you will understand. We're going to take your video camera away from you for two weeks."

"You can't do that to me!" Dawson said. "I need my camera for the film class at school."

"Why didn't you think about that on Friday, before you did this stupid thing?" Mr Leery said angrily. "You're the—" Then he stopped speaking suddenly. He looked at his wife. "That was terrible," he said. "I sound like my own father. He always said things like that to me when *I* was young and crazy."

"Dad, Mom," Dawson said. "It's OK. Take my camera. I'd like to tell you, 'I'll never do anything like that again.' But I'm a teenager with problems, and I'm trying to become an adult. So I probably *will* do more stupid things. But today, I'm very sorry."

"Oh, yes, you'll do many more stupid things—we're sure about that," Mr Leery said. He laughed. "And each time you do something stupid, we'll be here to punish you."

Dawson nodded his head. He wasn't unhappy about that idea. He got up and left the room.

———

Pacey was sitting in the living room of his father's house. His father knew all about the trip to New York. Doug Witter had returned from the police convention a day early. He had found out about Pacey's trip from Abby Morgan. Abby had enjoyed telling Doug about it. And Doug had enjoyed phoning his father with the news.

"You're a failure, Pacey," his father told him. "Everything in your life is wrong. Every choice you make is wrong. Why can't you be like your brother?"

"I'm sorry, Dad," Pacey said unhappily. "I won't do it again."

"Your apology isn't good enough," Mr Witter said angrily. "Why didn't you ask me about borrowing the truck?"

"Because you would have said no," said Pacey, simply.

"Well *that's* true!" Mr Witter said. "But you didn't ask. You stole the truck! While I've been at a convention about teenage criminals, you've *become* a teenage criminal. There's only one thing to do with you—there's only one thing that you'll understand. I'm going to arrest you. You'll be arrested for stealing. Maybe you'll go to jail. I can't help you any more, and—"

At that moment, the phone started to ring. Mr Witter picked it up.

"Yes, I'm Chief Witter," he said into the phone. Then he was quiet for a while. He was listening to someone who had something to tell him. After a few minutes, he spoke again. "Thank you for telling me about this," he said. "It was kind of you to call. Did my son ask you to call me? No, I understand. Goodbye."

Mr Witter put the phone down and he looked carefully at his son.

"That was a lady named Mrs Phyllis Hanover," he said. "She phoned to tell me about you and your friends. You were trying to get back here before I did. But you stopped to help her because she was in trouble. And she tried to give you some money, but you didn't take it. Well, maybe there is *something* good in you, son. Maybe you'll behave better one day."

"Are you going to arrest me, Dad?" Pacey asked quietly.

"No, I'm not going to arrest you," Mr Witter replied. "But I don't understand you, Pacey. I don't understand you at all."

"I don't understand me either, Dad," said Pacey. "But I apologize about the truck." And he left the room.

———

Late that evening, Joey picked up her phone. She called Dawson's number and he answered quickly.

"Hi, Dawson," Joey said. "I called to say goodnight. Are your parents very angry with you?"

"Well, I'm still alive," Dawson said. "They didn't kill me. Joey, listen to me. I need to tell you something. I do understand what you said about Danny. You saw him, and then your life changed. It happened to me too. I met a girl in a parking lot in Staten Island, and everything changed for me. She was a dancer and she was beautiful. I'll never see her again—I know that. But the world is a different place for me too."

"Why are you telling me this, Dawson?" Joey asked. She wasn't happy to hear about Dixie.

"I want to be honest with you, Joey," Dawson said. "You want us to be honest with each other. You want us to be honest about our feelings. You told me that."

Suddenly Joey felt better.

"Dawson," she whispered.

"Yes?"

"I only wanted to say your name. Goodnight."

And Joey smiled as she put the phone down.

Points for Understanding

1

1 Joey says, "Life isn't like a movie, Dawson." What does she mean?
2 Where does Jen invite Joey? Why? What does Joey think about this?

2

1 Why do Pacey and Dawson decide to go to New York?
2 Who hears them talking about their plans? What important information does this person learn?

3

1 Who do Jen and Joey meet at The Cellar?
2 What are the girls' feelings about these people?
3 How do these people behave? Give your opinion.

4

Why does Dawson's life change at six thirty on Saturday morning?

5

1 What do Joey and Jen do on Saturday morning?
2 Who do they meet? What does this person say?
3 What happens at Capeside on Saturday evening?

6

1 What big surprise do the girls find outside the apartment?
2 Why isn't Jen surprised by the Rose Room at the Plaza Hotel?

7

1 At the Plaza Hotel, a young woman speaks to Dawson and Pacey. "Maybe you've come to the wrong party," she says. Why does she think this?

2 Joey tells Jen's aunt, "I invited them (Pacey and Dawson) here." This is not true. Why does Joey say it?

8

1 "Why do I worry about behaving badly?" Pacey asks himself. Why does he ask himself this question?

2 Pacey, Jen, and Mrs Hanover are going to look for a garage. Why do they have to do this?

9

1 When Dawson enters the living room of his house, he guesses something. What does he guess? Why does he believe this?

2 "Well, maybe there is something good in you, son," Mr Witter says to Pacey. Why does he say this?

Other

Dawson's Creek ™

stories in the Macmillan Guided Readers Series
at Elementary Level:

Dawson's Creek: The Beginning of Everything Else

Jennifer Baker
Based on teleplays by Kevin Williamson
Retold by F. H. Cornish

Kevin Williamson, creator of the highly popular TV show, "Dawson's Creek™" has also written highly successful feature films (*Scream, I Know What You Did Last Summer, Scream 2*) and marked his directorial debut with his own screenplay, *Teaching Mrs Tingle*. "Dawson's Creek™" has been shown in more than 50 countries around the world. The popularity of the show is proven by its huge fanbase. Members of the young cast have gone on to star in successful feature films.

In this specially adapted version of the story which formed the pilot and first episode of the TV show written by Kevin Williamson, we are introduced to four young residents of the town of Capeside who attend the same high school. The teenagers all have similar hopes, fears and ambitions. The trouble is that love, school work and parents often make things more complicated.

Joey Potter knows that she and Dawson Leery cannot continue their relationship on "best friend" terms forever. Will Dawson ever love her the way she loves him, particularly as he is attracted to newcomer, Jen Lindley? But Jen has entered the small coastal community with a troubled past. Meanwhile charming, funny Pacey Witter is constantly at odds—with his school teachers, his family, and with life in general.

64pp

   0 333 97314 3

   0 333 97315 1

   0 333 97316 X